Tattooed

Tattooed

Poems

Carine Topal

Palettes & Quills
Rochester, NY

Palettes & Quills

1935 Penfield Road
Penfield, NY 14526
http://www.palettesnquills.com/
dmmarbach@gmail.com

Publisher: Donna M. Marbach
Book Design and Layout: Tom Holmes

Cover Image: "The Abyss" by Diana Paul

ISBN 10: 0-9888092-1-4
ISBN 13: 978-0-9888092-1-5

Printed in the United States.

9-30-15
La Quinta / CA

FOR Linda ("Linda Lovey")

Thank you for point-
ing me in a healthier
direction, for saving my marriage,
and myself.

With love + gratitude,
Carine

Table of Contents

Introduction

Carine Topal's *Tattooed* is the 2014 winner of an international poetry chapbook competition judged by poet Kelly Cherry and sponsored by Palettes & Quills.

Tattooed is Palettes & Quills fourth effort at sponsoring a contest and publishing a single-poet chapbook. Like all publishing projects, production of this chapbook required the help and participation of numerous individuals, including over 100 other poets who competed in this contest. Thus, I want to give special thanks to all those poets across the U. S. and overseas, who shared their work with us. There were many excellent manuscripts several of which have been picked up and published by other publishers and still others I am certain will be snatched up shortly.

I also want to thank our first readers, all excellent poets themselves, who spent endless hours reading, sorting, commenting on, and ranking all submissions: Ron Bailey, Ann Putnam, Anita Augsesen, and Kathleen Van Schaick. I also thank Carol McMahon, our MFA Intern who assisted with second level readings , and Tom Holmes (editor of *Redactions: Poetry & Poetics)* who helped in many ways from promotional outreach, through marketing advice, to design and layout of the final book.

Finally, I want to extend a very big thank you to Kelly Cherry, who was patent, flexible, and a delight to work with. In addition, she took time out from a busy holiday schedule to thoroughly review and carefully assess each manuscript sent her.

Donna M. Marbach
Publisher

My Back Story: Family History

In 1972, while living in Germany, I visited Dachau Concentration Camp. My mother was born in Germany and fled at the height of the Third Reich, when she was 16, in 1938. I heard many stories about her life as a Jew in Germany, and I had inherited some of my fears as a result of her treatment in the 1930s. On several occasions, I have been a target of anti-Semitism, here, in the United States. Of course, I make no comparisons.

In 2012, I travelled to Poland and visited the site of the Aushcwitz Concentration Camp. My Aunt Lola (my mother's first cousin with whom I lived over the years in Israel) as well as her parents, two brothers, and a younger sister were sent to Auschwitz in early 1940. Only one-and-half years before, my mother and grandfather took the train from Dresden, Germany, to Benjzin, Poland, to encourage his sister and her family to leave Poland. They refused, believing that they were in little danger. Only Lola would survive Auschwitz. That was the story I was told. I knew little more. My Aunt never spoke of the camps to her two children, or to anyone else. But in 1998 she agreed to do an interview with the Shoah Foundation. She told her story in its entirety. I write this book for her and all of those who were murdered in the most horrid of killing machines.

This book is dedicated to my Aunt Lola, Auschwitz survivor,
And to her Brothers, Sister and Parents who perished there.
And to the 11,000,000 Jews, Gypsies, Poles, homosexuals, and
political prisoners who can no longer tell this story.
And to my mother who fled, just in time.

Tattooed

We Were Going Somewhere, 1939

I was on my knees and scuttled, if there's a word for what I did and how they saw me — what I seemed, there on the floor of pine needles and autumn — where I almost fell into song. I so loved the taste of November, the month my mother, a pale redhead afraid of fire and birds, emerged from her mother in a hospital on a tree-lined street, in a country split in half, speaking a guttural tongue. By the time her family caught wind of conspiracy, of scapegoat, of yellow stars, *hurry* she shouted at birth, as if time moved forward without history and she and millions of others left the room, valises bound with rope, hands gloved against a cold wind at the dock. And the ship left with her, a taffeta gown, a chandelier and glass tea cups, sailing to some place, going some where

The Season In Which We Carried All That We Owned

Our men wore long black coats to hide
whatever they'd need inside.
We packed the shoes good for walking
though we were going by train.

A Survivor Remembers The Arrival

Small fortunes neatly placed in rows. From where I stood they looked like tender headstones. Then, later, ribbons tied to a pair of small shoes. Small red shoes. Each of us brought a bundle, valise or satchel marked with name, street, and city: *Goldstein Sara Nadelmann Clara.* While waiting in line we asked one another *should we hold the bundle or let it go, travel lighter?* There comes a time when mercy is not called for, this being the time to run, to pick up stones. Something to wield, to hold on to, to wonder, *have we not come to the wrong town, taken the wrong train?*

Shoes

Dedicated to Doris Mathes
Born June 14, 1942
Gassed January 17, 1944

Cork-soled, peep-toe, half-boots, heavy flannel.
First shoes – nested where the train stopped, after
it pulled thousands through, the scale of it cruel,
ash grey, brick red, russet, black, bone, amber.

But the tiny shoes, from the smallest limbs,
at the last stop – dare take your little one,
      have her try them on – walk where they were taken,
      pocket-sized ankle straps, buckles undone,

mounds of leather booties, blue marguerite.
      Such shoes, once stripped by winter, stripped of grace
long since buried in fields planted by grief.
      Now turn away from them, the shoes, their fate.

Exactly like that.
Exactly like that.

{Tattoo}

They pulled off my coat. It was not yet spring.
Snow covered the willow beside the guard tower.
Unforeseen, to find beauty here.

They offered me a seat then took my left hand as though
separate from my body, knuckles downward.
My wedding band had already been taken.

The officer with beautiful teeth glanced at my arm
and got to work, gripping a wrist that was no longer mine.
I made myself look hard at this,

the man beginning with number 3, staying there until it turned green,
and I bled and knew I was human, and knew the arm was mine.
It was good, that pain, so I stole another look in the hope

that more numbers would come, and they did, and the man threw
   back his head to laugh,
the needle neatly imbedded in my skin, his teeth
a perfect fence. He looked at the tattoo,

blew tenderly on the wound.
Silence fell upon him and he looked up at me
like someone who suddenly had something to say.

Auschwitz: (The Orchestra)

they dragged their bodies barefoot through shit –
shit to the waist, deep in wishes, deep in a tired thaw –
waist deep in wishes, shit, and the deep dragging in of ash
now silt, yet wishing to live on, these hearts cast
out – cut stone. Has our starving god mistaken this
stone for sustenance, given us the means for music, the which
for everything else? Whose twisted theater, whose music,
this sudden ictus
when the orchestra plays for time, while we tally such
grotesqueries – the walking dead honoring nothing – into the song
of what?

Birkenau: A Guard's Confession

He hated
how the willow next to the guard house
rubbed itself, its wood.

Hated their shoes
their gold teeth
   their blue-eyed babies
      the orchestra tapping out Mozart
        in striped pajamas,

hated how they balked at the *Judenrampe* –
overflowing with shoes, fur coats, and valises
   filled with oranges and soap –

hated the yelping dogs, the squadrons,
   the gates, the lineups,
how they turned away from the chimney's exhaust,
(how on earth)
the stench the smoke the ash. Hated
    the stock-piling of spectacles
    hair
    teeth

   The traffic inside this busy oven where the blood went through.
   The iron pathway that brought them here.

All The Birds Are Back Again (*Alle Vögel sind schon da*)

song played immediately before execution

In the kingdom of heaven's sake,
we played so we could live.

Lavender moths the size of our hands bobbed in the tangled
vines outside.

We were ordered to sing and we sang.
We even danced and carried on as if there were lines that could not
    be crossed,

crimes that could not be imagined. Wanting to hold on and to let go,
we started into a waltz,

into the leaking moonlight slowly sucking up
the sky.

German shepherds wound around the SS feet. Men marched, a few
carrying a body. No one begged for air.

The pink twilight was hours gone.
Never a bird – just the fugitive sorrow that followed.

Winter: Roll Call

I
Winter in our thin clothes. Our wooden
shoes, and always the smell of burning.
The snow that buried us to our knees,

the willing feet of Mengele's twins
their hair curly and long –
those who still resembled humans.

And their proper clothes:
the tartan jumper, the bright hat, the blue
shirt that shouted out to us –

the sad left dragging our own shadows –
which was what we heard the rabbi's wife whisper.
We thought the twins the lucky few,
those chosen in two's and fed biscuits and sugar cubes.
The rest of us stood for hours to be counted.

This is where we stood. Shoeless in winter.
Slender willow and birch staring us down.

II

In spring there will be traces of grass here and there.
If we are lucky, a bird.

Yesterday I stole a girl's scarf.
I'd do that again. That is what I'd do.
Yesterday she had a mouthful of tiny teeth, which today
are missing. There is no end to my wanting.

When I marry, I want to have children. When I dream, I dream
of giving birth to birds. Then I witness myself dead. Faith is
   impossible.

If we could lose ourselves in snow, in the changeling dark,
flecks of bone ground down to calcium,
we could feed these grueling fields.

Interrogation: {Confession}

I'm not a Jew who looks back at his failures and asks of himself
what the long night asks of him.

I'm not a Jew, no half-gypsy, no low down lover of other men or
    kinder
no rigged man of religion, not

for Christ's sake, the brother of a priest whose mother, left in the
    forsaken fields
to fend for herself, lies down in those fields. And not

the cousin who, with dirty nails, stands in a broad road holding
three eggs staring straight at the sky into the future.

I never hid a Jew, never touched the yellow star on his threadbare coat
and called him *mein Freund,*

            and if I had, we never spoke of it, never whispered
words that rang untrue or small.

I'm not the slick-haired Yid with a purse filled with *pfennings*
not a liar using guile to hide my yellow star,

my backbone perfectly carved, alabaster bone of your own conviction.
Not the dark curtain of your knowing.

I'm the certainty of the answer, when the long night asks
is this what became of sin?

A Medical Confession

i {The Instruments}

> Picture two sterile clamps on a background of linen,
> how they tie off the blood vessels
> at either end mimicking a combat wound.
> As if you could have imagined this.

Here are his dissecting scissors – curved or round –
the needles, the polished blades, tubes, forceps,
the small bone mallet, the pliers, scalpel,
sutures, the disinfected knives suggesting mirrors, vials, vats, and
   gloves.

Tools of the trade.

ii {The Dissecting Room}

You must imagine a room bathed in light.
    Whitewashed . Well lit. Sterile.

One large window overlooks a birch grove.

The concrete floor is red –
    the color of a heart.

In the center of the room   a table of polished marble.
    Along its edges, several drains for the bleeding.

Against the wall, three porcelain sinks, and the second window, above
   the table
    covered with a screen to keep out the flies.

The doctor holds a small head in one hand, documents the darkness
    of the hair in the other. The distance between the brows. The
    circumference of the head.

And staring up at Mengele with dead gimlet eyes, the very blossom
  of mercy.
    This gypsy boy.

Like a temple this child.
    This child like a temple.

iii {Pain Management: Surgery Without Anesthesia}

Once his spine had been snapped
      he was carried back to me, unable to walk.
In the morning, Mengele returned to open him up.
      His liver punctured   removed.
Other organs   tucked beneath organs   rearranged,
      infected ones gangrened and buried themselves in the maze
         of his belly.
Cat gut ligatures sewed up by Mengele closed my brother's open heart.
      Mine was beating in the next room.

My brother of tissue and bone   welts and open wounds
      slit, lacerated, hacked then gutted until hollow.

Dark puddles of blood pooled beneath a table,
      some spilled from vials on the sill where the fogged light
         came in.

Numbered among Mengele's sins,
      my twin, Tibi.

for Tibi and Moshe Offer

iv {Genetics}

Should we sew them up as one
    back to back, wrist to wrist
– the gypsy twins –
    or let them go
hollering in one voice
    cold into the oven?

 Should we study their likeness
    flush as petals
dressed in matching clothes
    – pockets filled with bonbons –
or draw a distinction between the two
    inject the methylene to make one's black eyes blue
then settle the second one in
    with the sweet smell of liquid,
and chloroform his beating heart?

for Guido and Nino, age 4

v {Hypothermia: Cold Exposure and Rewarming}

the body prepares itself for winter

A long view of the grieving brain
indicates a cluster of crooked blossoms
waxy from a mock winter in which the Jew froze.

The first chimes of hypothermia purpled the medulla
and stripped him of breath.
How long did it take the body to warm?

And what killed him after freezing in a bath of snow?
Was he thawed too quickly, was it the glycerin
injected throughout the afternoon hours or was it

his arms and neck ticked with shots of lead that shut him down?
Was it the boiling tub meant to warm him
or the heat from the borrowed light of a dozen sun lamps

crisping his skin? Or surely it was the shock of the woman
brought in to fuck the frozen Jew
hour after hour in the hopes of warming him up.

How long did that take, and how was it that her body – flanked
by frozen flesh – stayed warm, as she attached herself, like an embrace,
to the cold armor of his body, hoping to save one of them?

for Mark and Francesca Berkowitz

Bone Jar: The Oven {An Elegy}

In the oven's arms, finger bones:
      distal, proximal.

On the highest flame, a child's velvet nape,
      the satiny small-boned vault

of a nail bed, skin's fingerprint melting.

Here's to the dirge of backbones
      simmering in concert with the femurs –

those longest of bones efficiently arranged.

      Here are the ribs, all 24 caged in the bony thoracic,
      and there the two floating, untethered from the sternum –

like starlings coming suddenly loose –
      letting at last go,

as though the structure of the world, encouraged to burn itself,
      gave in to resilience forever

And remember the stirrup bone, the stapes, most small of all
      taking in the crack and split

which could be heard as heartbreak:

Or it's the clavicle that once cinched a throat. Or a scapula.

And there's the din of the slow giving in of wishbones, millions deep.

1944: A Boy Dreams His Father's Escape

In the dream where you are walking,
all of what you carry flies away:
your striped coat. The yellow patch.

To the west: stars and the moon.

You are far from a border
surrounded by snow-capped mountains.
I kiss you from a distance.

Cloud to ground the smell of wet moss,

and somewhere an early winter thunderstorm.
An injured goat roams free,
but you wander further into the cold,
walking dead into it.

This is when I shiver

as I remember you
as you were, in a park
on a bench, feeding a bird.

The sound of limbs snapping under ice.

Peasant's Confession

Dabrowa Tarnowska-a county in southeastern Poland, 1942

It seems the Jew had stayed on since the rains of April.

He stirred in the long grass. On the damp land. I saw him while gathering broom-straw — sprigs of straw that I tied together with colored cloth. I saw hands and swollen feet moving toward a clearing, leaving footprints — mud locking in to the small spaces under his feet — which looked cloven.

Then the Jew lifted his head when he saw me and appeared to sing. I swear the sun around him shined and the grass sparkled. For days I watched the bandit daven and sway in the light. For days I watched how the sheen worked its way around the stunned Jew, as if light devised itself on all sides of him. Then he wailed — long slow cries. Then the glee. He was free after all.

I grew afraid, closed my window and lost sight of him for weeks. Neighbors say the children rode on the back of this broken shape, then force-fed him milkweed and bones — bones dug deep into the soil — to kill his thirst.

Sobriquet

It used to be grief who kept me whole, who knew my blood type, who stood at the foot of my bed. And I let it. Grief was a thing with shape and presence. I knew where I needed to be. It told me to feel safe so it could find me, as if it knew the future would be this way. And it told me so.

These days I sip from my own cup of kindness, ask myself if I'd like another, want veined by fits of joy. I'm built of nails, watch myself looking back at what I've done, carry the beautiful and the ugly like a signal of truth. Once released into pale sunlight, I do my chores. Forgive myself in secret. *Fond lamb.*

One foot's in winter – the invisible bridge covered in fog – thank god no one is jumping today. On the safe side, children giggling, holding hands, their waists tethered by rope, one to the next, while a woman, who looks like their mother, talks them through vapor circling their heads – like moving halos – the beauty of that, of what goes on without me.

Smaller Kingdoms

This was April. April tundra, and who could keep warm,
when Spring garlic still worked its way up, tipped its green
through the ice? When we ate only what we could carry.

This was when violets purpled between rock and sleeves
of cold. Who could leave here. Who could?

This was when the boy with a head like a lark sang like one,
demented with elaborate calm. It was singing difficult
to watch as his tiny winged shoulders flailed, and this
when he flew hungry into song.

And this when his sister saw Shakespeare in the moon
or it was quill and ink by window light, a glowing beneath
a lantern on a makeshift desk. When those tragedies
were written.

When our hungry fathers, who did the ancestors' dismal jobs,
craved smaller kingdoms, more easily managed. When my
father believed in the steady work of the living.

And this was when I walked around in my mother's body
like a long twilight of faith, because the small cleave to the
lowest branches – and where's the god in that?

Someone You Know

More than the dove, more than the mulberry
It's me that autumn loves. Gives me a veil.
"Take this for dreaming, "says its stitchery.
And: "God's as nearby as the vulture's nail."
                    – Paul Celan from "The Lonely One"

Not the snow, the frost: veil over mouth.
Not the dust, not the barracks in moonlight.
Not the wind, the smoke, the ash on the sill:
someone you know? Not the lightheaded women
at the window listening in their heads,
waiting for what? For the angels to arrive in a hurry.
For the garments you wore in a world you once knew:
a table with candle flame, an opus in a half-lit room:
your grand piano, your husband and child, such beauty,
more than the dove, more than the mulberry.

He is the field, the flood the law breaking itself.
He is the small sack of salt, the deluge confined
to no peril, the foot of Moses on the temple door.
He is the God, after all. He is the God!
See for yourself how the world turns and the news comes
by cattle car, by helmets and cross belts and boots. Inhale
beyond what is carted off. We are ankle deep in it, digging
our graves, burying our bones where his hand begins.
Cover us, the still living, hear our wail,
It's me that autumn loves. Gives me a veil.

Let me look to the icy blackness – through the evening's
dark by this window of lingering widows – to be somewhere
other than where I am, which is no country at all, that I might
sleep a painless sleep in a district drunk with stars,
ungovernable on the outskirts of a far-flung township, whose
waving flag remains in the shadows of this remote humility.
Take my panicked feet married to the barrack floor, centuries
of being summoned to a transitory patch of land.
Deliver us our fragmentary scroll. Mend our deficiency,
"Take this for dreaming," says its stitchery.

Among the signs which spelled disaster, our family – dismantled –
in lines to the left or the right. Among the exiles at your back,
 a million shoes off the feet of children, mothers tilting their heads
toward the world which is no longer their world. For you the earth
of cloistered exits is a temple. Our shoes in piles – our tomb unveiled.
Appear somehow among the waste facing the world's secret injuries.
As if we mattered, dress us in cast-off overcoats that we may leave
this life behind, though this is no life. And show yourself to some avail,
As: "God's as nearby as the vulture's nail."

Author's Biography

Carine Topal, a native New Yorker, writes and teaches in Los Angeles and the desert area. She has lived in Jerusalem, Israel, where she worked with Palestinian merchants. She was also employed by the Office of Assimilation, and worked with Morrocan Jews. She has also lived in Germany on the American army base in Heidelberg. Since 1982, she has anthologized the poetry of special needs children. She  participated in the grassroots organization California Poets in the Schools, was the Poet-in-Residence for the city of Manhattan Beach and Poet-in-Education for Manhattan Beach elementary schools. In 1994, her first collection of poetry, *God As Thief*, was published by The Amagansett Press. Her work has appeared in numerous journals throughout the U.S. and Canada. In 2004, she was nominated for a Pushcart Prize, and in 2005, awarded a residency at Hedgebrook, as well as a fellowship in St. Petersburg, Russia. In 2006, Carine conducted poetry workshops at the VA Hospital in Los Angeles. She is the recipient of numerous poetry awards, including the 2007 Robert G. Cohn Prose Poetry Award from California Arts and Letters, from which a special edition chapbook *Bed of Want* was published. Her third collection of poetry, *In the Heaven of Never Before*, was published in December, 2008, by Moon Tide Press. In 2008, Carine was honored with the Excellence in Arts Award from the Cultural Arts Commission of Torrance, California. Carine has traveled extensively throughout Israel, Palestinian territories, Cuba, Mexico, Poland, and Russia. Currently, she teaches memoir and poetry workshops in Redondo Beach and Palm Springs, California.

Acknowledgments

Briar Cliff Review
    Someone You Know

Caliban Online
    We Were Going Somewhere, 1939
    Desertion
    The Disssecting Room

Spoon River Poetry Review
    Bone Jar: The Oven {An Elegy}

The Touchstone
    Birkenau
    {Tattoo}

Much gratitude to Laurel-Anne Bosselaar, who pushed me through these poems, and Cecilia Woloch, who made them possible. Thanks to Dorothy Barresi and her workshop poets for their good guidance: Brenda Yates, Candace Pearson, Cathie Sandstrom, Judith Pacht, Kate Hovey, Keven Bellows, Lynne Thompson, and Mary Fitzpatrick.

First Readers' Biographies

ANITA AUGESEN is a retired career counselor and poet. She hosts the open mic for Just Poets, a large nonprofit poetry group in Rochester, NY. Her poems appear in many journals and anthologies, including *Le Mot Juste, Knocking on the Silence, Summer Songs, Remembering Faces*, and *Liberty's Virgil*. Augesen is also a photographer/artist and her works have been exhibited in local galleries.

RON BAILEY was born in Syracuse, NY, and went to college to become a teacher of English and Creative Writing He taught for thirty-three years in public, private, and college settings, and still teaches at Writers & Books, a nonprofit literary organization in Rochester, NY. Along the way, he has published a number of poems in many publications and authored a chapbook in 2001.

CAROL MCMAHON is a teacher and poet. She is also an avid reader and writer with poems published in several journals, including *Haz-Mat, Lake Affect Magazine*, and *Blue Collar Review*, and in anthologies, such as *Le Mot Juste*, and she is also the author of the chapbook *On Any Given Day* (FootHills Publishing). Carol is currently working on her MFA in Creative Writing from the Rainier Writing Workshop.

ANN PUTNAM, now retired, worked for many years in high school administration. Her work has been published in *Lucidity, Borderlines, Le Mot Juste, ByLine ,The Aurorean, Poet Talk* and *Pencil Marks*. She has also been a featured reader for Just Poets, the RochesterInk poetry series, and for the Genesee Reading Series at Writer's & Books.

KATHLEEN VAN SCHAICK, a retired elementary school teacher, was an editor for the *Le Mot Juste* anthologies from 2008 to 2010. Her work has been published in *The MacGuffin, The Broad River Review, Cairn: St. Andrews Review, The Dire Elegies: 59 Poets on Endangered Species of North America*, and *Listening to Water: The Susquehanna Watershed Anthology*. She was awarded the 2006 Portia Steele Award in Poetry sponsored by the San Francisco Peninsula chapter of the California Writers Club and has read her poetry at many local venues.

Final Judge's Biography

KELLY CHERRY has previously published twenty-one books (novels, stories, poetry, memoir, criticism, and reviews), nine chapbooks, and two translations of classical drama. In spring 2014 the University of Wisconsin Press will publish her new collection of interlinked stories titled *A Kind of Dream*. Her newest full-length collection of poems, *The Life and Death of Poetry*, was published by LSU Press in 2013 and her newest chapbook, a group of poems titled *Vectors*, appeared from Parallel Press in December 2012. She was the first recipient of the Hanes Poetry Prize given by the Fellowship of Southern Writers for a body of work. Other awards include fellowships from the National Endowment for the Arts, the Rockefeller Foundation, the Bradley Major Achievement (Lifetime) Award, a USIS Speaker Award (The Philippines), a Distinguished Alumnus Award, three Wisconsin Arts Board fellowships, two WAB New Work awards, the Dictionary of Literary Biography Yearbook Award for Distinguished Book of Stories in 1999 (2000), and selection as a Wisconsin Notable Author. Her stories have also appeared in *Best American Short Stories, The O. Henry Awards: Stories, The Pushcart Prize*, and *New Stories from the South*. In 2010, she was a Director's Visitor at the Institute for Advanced Study in Princeton. In 2012, she received both the Taramuto Prize for a story and the Carole Weinstein Prize for Poetry. In 2013 she received the L. E. Phillabaum Award for Poetry. Former Poet Laureate of Virginia, she is Eudora Welty Professor Emerita of English and Evjue-Bascom Professor Emerita in the Humanities at the University of Wisconsin-Madison. She and her husband live in Virginia.

About the Cover Artwork

"The Abyss" is a 9" x 13" collagraph depicting a primal void, a nightmare of chaos, before awakening and renewal.

Artist Diana Paul has two passions: printmaking and writing. For her, both require careful composing, revealing in clean muted tones and in an understated, elegant way, an illusionist's window bridging language and image. For Paul, these two creative processes – one visual, the other verbal – are intertwined. In Paul's upcoming novel, *Things Unsaid*, as well as in her mixed media prints, the reader/viewer is given a chance to alter preconceived notions about our visual and emotional world.

Colophon

The typeface used for the text pages is Joanna, which has been called the most engaging of Eric Gill's typefaces. The design was drawn by Gill and first cut in 1931 by the Caslon foundry for the exclusive use of Gill's printing firm, Hague & Gill. This hand-set version of the typeface was only made available in two sizes and, fittingly, the first use of the font was to set Gill's own "Essay on Typography." Not long after, Hague & Gill was acquired by J. M. Dent & Sons, and the rights to Joanna came along with it. In 1937, Monotype produced a machine-set version for the exclusive use of Joanna's new owner, but Dent later agreed to a general release of the small family of roman and italic designs, at which time Monotype added these fonts to their prestigious typeface library. He created the typeface for the printing firm of Hague & Gill, which he formed to give his idle son-in-law an occupation, and named the design for his daughter. Only the Caslon foundry cut it for hand composition. It is, as Gill himself described it, "a book face free from all fancy business," with small, straight serifs and a spare elegance that makes it notably attractive and distinguished.

The type face for the cover is Charlemagne Std. During the reign of the Emperor Charlemagne in the eighth and ninth centuries, the use of classical roman letterforms was revived. These letterforms were the basis of the highly refined versal capitals of late tenth-century England, which were the inspiration for Carol Twombly's 1989 Adobe Originals typeface. Charlemagne has spiky serifs, but retains clean lines and proportions.

ABOUT PALETTES & QUILLS

Founded in 2002, Palettes & Quills is devoted to the celebration and expansion of the literary and visual arts, offering both commissioned and consulting services. It works to support beginning and emerging writers and artists to expand their knowledge, improve their skills, and connect to other resources in the community. Further, Palettes & Quills seeks to increase the public's awareness and appreciation of these arts through education, advocacy, hands-on assistance, and by functioning as a literary press.

Palettes & Quills Titles include:
* *Conversations with the Poet* ($6.00) anthology
* *Remembering Faces* ($10.00) anthology
* *When She's Asked to Think of Colors* ($10.00) by Katharyn Howd Machan *
* *Cinquainicity* ($10.00) anthology
* *Pure Elysium* ($10.00) by Michael Meyerhofer*
* *When Tigers Do Not Come* ($10.00) by Meg Cowan*
* *Poems For an Empty Church* ($15.00) by Tom Holmes

* Chapbook Contest Winners

Broadsides by David Michael Nixon inlude:
* The Green Turtle Dream ($3.00)
› The Thinning Sheet ($3.00)
› Live as Always (St. Francis Addresses the Birds) ($3.00)

For more information or to order, contact:
Palettes & Quills
1935 Penfield Road
Penfield, 14526
Phone: 585-383-0812
Email: *dmmarbach@gmail.com*
Submissions Email: *palettesnquills@gmail.com*
Website: *www.palettesnquills.com*

Tattooed